From Clicks To Customers

Turning your Dance Website Into a Student Enrollment Machine

Stephen Reinstein

Dedication

To the incredible team at Market Muscles, Your dedication, creativity, and hard work make it possible for us to fulfill our mission of connecting millions of children with dance and martial arts studios. This book, like our success, is a testament to your commitment and talent. Thank you for bringing our vision to life every day.

To my girlfriend, Cindy, Your unwavering support has been my foundation as I pursue my passion through Market Muscles. Your encouragement and understanding have made this journey possible.

To my best friend, Cris, Your constant guidance and support, both in business and in life, have been invaluable. Your wisdom and friendship have shaped not only this book but also the person I've become. Thank you for always being there.

To all my mentors and those who came before me, Your shared knowledge and support have been instrumental in shaping who I am today. Thank you for your guidance and for paving the way. I stand on the shoulders of giants.

And to all the studio owners and instructors who dedicate their lives to enriching children's lives through dance and martial arts. Your passion inspires our work every day.

Contents

Introduction

My name is Stephen Reinstein, and my journey to becoming a marketing expert for dance and martial arts studios is both unexpected and deeply personal. It all began when I was just three years old, thrust into the world of martial arts because that's what the rest of my family was doing. Little did I know then how this forced activity would become my anchor in a sea of change.

Life wasn't always straightforward for me. My parents divorced when I was 12, setting off a series of challenging life changes. At 13, I found myself living with family friends. Later, I faced the harsh reality of an abusive, drug-addicted stepfather. I eventually moved back in with my dad, stepmom, two brothers, and four stepbrothers. Picture this: nine of us crammed into a three-bedroom house, all boys sharing one bathroom. It was chaotic, but it was home.

It was in this bustling household that I discovered my love for computers. Thanks to my dad, who wrote books for Microsoft, I'd grown up with technology since I was five. This early exposure sparked a passion that would shape my future.

At 16, I made a bold decision – I dropped out of high school to pursue my true passion: websites and marketing. It was a risky move, but I knew in my gut that this was my path.

One thing remained constant throughout these changes: martial arts and my instructor. This discipline and mentorship gave me the stability and life skills to persevere through the most challenging times. This experience connects me deeply to what dance studio owners do every day.

I know that every dance instructor out there is doing for their students exactly what my martial arts teacher did for me. You're not just teaching steps or movements; you're shaping lives, building confidence, and providing a safe haven for kids who might be facing their own challenges at home. It can often feel like a thankless job, but trust me, your impact is immeasurable. For kids like me, you're not just instructors – you're lifelines.

This realization became my driving force. Eight years ago, I founded Market Muscles with a mission to connect kids like me to studios like yours. It started with building a website for my instructor and watching his phone light up with notifications of new leads.

From that moment, I knew I had created something special – a tool that could help dance and martial arts studios everywhere grow and thrive. Fast forward eight years, and we're now serving over a thousand studios, connecting more than 1.5 million families to these life-changing programs.

But the story doesn't end there. As martial arts school owners started referring their friends who own dance studios, we realized that our strategies could revolutionize the dance world, too. We began applying the same website and marketing techniques to dance studios, and the results have been nothing short of spectacular.

In this book, I'm sharing the exact techniques and strategies we use to build websites that convert effectively – the same ones that have helped studios worldwide see massive growth. These aren't just marketing tactics; they're the result of a personal journey that taught me the true value of what you do.

So, as we dive into these strategies, remember: we're not just talking about websites and lead generation. We're talking about creating more opportunities for children to find their anchor, confidence, and passion – just like I did. Together, we're going to turn your website into a powerful tool that doesn't just grow your studio but changes lives, one student at a time.

Getting Started

Picture this: You've invested significant time and resources into creating an impressive website for your dance studio. It's packed with detailed calendars, student spotlights, and extensive information. However, your website might not be as effective as it could be.

Let's be honest: many of us have been treating our websites like online bulletin boards. But here's a crucial insight – your website isn't primarily for your current students or their parents. Take a moment to let that sink in.

Your website should be the digital gateway for potential new students, not a resource hub for your current dance community. That's what parent portals and student dashboards are for. Your website's primary job is to convert curious visitors into eager new students.

Think of your website as your studio's top performer, always ready to impress and engage new audiences. It's not there to remind current students about upcoming events. Instead, your website should be actively working to attract new students who are ready to discover their passion for dance.

This shift in perspective is vital. It's the difference between a website that's merely informative and one that's a powerful recruitment tool. It's time to transform your website from a passive information repository into an active enrollment generator.

Are you ready to make your website the most effective member of your studio staff? Great! Let's explore the world of conversion-focused web design. By the end of this book, your website will be outperforming the competition, and your studio will be welcoming a steady stream of new students.

Now that we've adjusted our mindset, let's talk about conversion rates – the key metric for measuring your website's effectiveness.

Imagine your website as a busy reception area. People are coming in, looking around, and deciding whether to sign up. In digital terms, we call this traffic. But here's the exciting part: a high-performing website doesn't just attract visitors; it persuades them to take action.

An optimized dance studio website should be converting 5-15% of all its visitors into leads. That means for every 100 people who visit your website, 5 to 15 of them should be leaving their contact details, expressing interest in your classes.

If you're thinking, "But my website barely gets any leads!" don't worry – you're not alone. This potential goldmine is an untapped resource for most dance studios. It's like discovering a hidden opportunity you never knew existed.

Let's break it down numerically: If your website gets 1,000 visitors a month, a 10% conversion rate means 100 new leads. Even if only 20% of those leads become students, that's 20 new dancers. Over a year, that could translate to 140 potential new students.

Even with a more conservative estimate of 120 additional new students per year, that's still enough to fill several new classes or justify expanding your studio.

The best part? These aren't just random leads. These are people who have actively sought out your studio, connected with your online presence, and taken the first step to join your dance community. They're high-quality leads, ready for you to engage.

Are you ready to transform your website into a powerful marketing tool? By the time we're done, your website will be working efficiently to bring in a steady stream of eager new students ready to pursue their dance aspirations with you.

Let's get started on redesigning a website that doesn't just participate in the digital landscape – it excels.

1. Overall Structure: This is your website's posture. We'll ensure it stands tall and proud, with a logo that catches the eye, navigation smoother than a glissade, and a call-to-action that's impossible to ignore.

2. Photos & Videos That Build Connection: Because a picture is worth a thousand words, but the right picture is worth a thousand leads. We'll show you how to choose visuals that make prospects want to leap through their screens and into your studio.

3. Leverage Social Proof to Boost Confidence: We're talking testimonials that pack more punch than a perfectly executed grand jeté. You'll learn to showcase your studio's greatest hits without sending visitors off on a social media tangent.

4. Age-Based Class Pages for Clarity: No more confusion for parents wondering if their 7-year-old belongs in the "Teeny Twirlers" or "Junior Jumpers." We'll create crystal-clear pathways for every age group, turning bewildered browsers into confident enrollees.

5. Community Recognition & Awards: It's time to toot your own horn (or blow your own whistle, if that's more your style). We'll help you showcase your studio's star power and community impact, making you the obvious choice for dance education.

6. Set Yourself Apart with Your Unique Culture: Your studio isn't just four walls and a barre – it's a unique blend of passion, values, and pizzazz. We'll help you communicate your special sauce, attracting students who are ready to dive into your studio culture headfirst.

7. The Missing Link for 98% of Studios: Prepare for a plot twist that'll make your head spin faster than a fouetté. We're about to challenge everything you thought you knew about displaying pricing and schedules online.

Spoiler alert: less is more, and mystery leads to enrollment.

Each of these points is powerful on its own, but when combined, they create a website that's truly compelling. We're not just talking about minor adjustments here – we're planning a comprehensive website overhaul that will significantly boost your online presence and effectiveness.

So, get ready to enhance your website-building skills and expand your digital marketing expertise. By the time we work through these seven points, your website will be attracting leads at an impressive rate. Are you ready to transform your website into a standout success? Let's get started!

Website Structure

Mobile Responsiveness

In today's digital age, your website needs to be highly adaptable. Why? Because over 65% of your website visitors are accessing your site via mobile devices. That's right - based on the data from thousands of websites we maintain, more than two-thirds of your potential students are checking out your studio on their smartphones or tablets.

This means that having a mobile-responsive website isn't just an optional feature - it's an absolute necessity. Your website should look as impressive and function as smoothly on a small phone screen as it does on a large desktop monitor.

Think of it this way: if your website doesn't perform well on mobile, it's like having a beautiful studio with a door that's too narrow for most people to enter. You're potentially turning away more than half of your prospects before they even get to see what you offer!

Here are a few key points to consider for mobile responsiveness:

1. Fluid layouts: Your website should automatically adjust to fit any screen size.

2. Touch-friendly navigation: Buttons and links should be large enough to tap easily with a finger.

3. Fast loading times: Mobile users often have less patience for slow-loading pages.

4. Readable text: Font sizes should be comfortable to read without zooming.

5. Optimized images: Pictures should look crisp on high-resolution mobile screens without slowing down the site.

Remember, your mobile site isn't a simplified version of your desktop site. It should offer the full experience, just packaged differently. All the crucial elements - your compelling photos, clear class information, and that all-important call-to-action - need to be front and center on mobile too.

By ensuring your website performs excellently on mobile devices, you're making sure that no matter how potential students find you - whether they're browsing on their lunch break or scrolling before bed - they'll have a seamless, engaging experience that makes them want to immediately visit your studio.

So, as we go through the rest of this book's strategies, keep mobile in mind. After all, in the world of digital marketing, mobile responsiveness is the key feature that will elevate your studio above the competition.

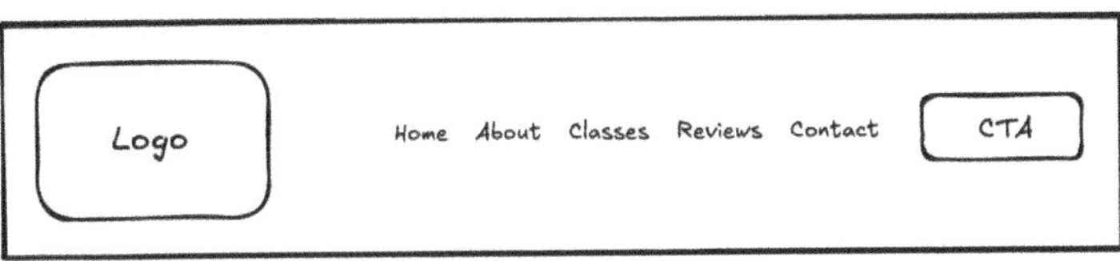

Logo Placement and Branding

Let's start with a crucial element of your studio's visual identity: your logo and branding.

Think of your logo as the star performer of your website. It needs to be prominent, catching attention the moment the page loads. But where exactly should this key element be positioned?

Top left is the ideal spot. It's the digital equivalent of a prime starting position—classic, reliable, and always effective. This is where Western eyes naturally begin their online journey. Your logo should be proudly displayed in this prime real estate, ready to make an immediate impression.

But remember, size matters here. Your logo should be like a well-executed performance—noticeable without being overwhelming. Aim for the right balance: not so small that it gets overlooked, but not so large that it overshadows the rest of your site's elements.

Now, let's talk about consistency. Your logo isn't a standalone element—it's part of your overall brand. This means your website's color scheme, fonts, and overall style should be in perfect harmony with your logo. Think of it as coordinating your entire site to the same theme.

Remember, your logo and branding are doing more than just looking attractive—they're telling your studio's story at a glance. They should evoke the feeling of your studio immediately. Are you focused on classical techniques? Modern fusion? High-energy styles? Your branding should communicate this to visitors before they've even scrolled down the page.

Lastly, don't be afraid to give your logo some breathing room. White space around your logo is like a moment of anticipation—it draws the eye and builds interest.

So, place that logo firmly in the top left corner, ensure it complements your overall branding, and watch as it helps turn your website into a lead-generating powerhouse. In your website's overall presentation, your logo sets the tone for everything that follows. Make it count!

Simple, Intuitive Navigation

Let's face it: if your website navigation is more complicated than a quadruple pirouette, you're in trouble. Your visitors should be able to glide through your site as smoothly as a dancer across a freshly waxed floor. So, let's break down the steps to create a navigation menu that's music to your visitors' eyes.

First things first: Keep it simple, sweetie. We're talking minimalist chic, not cluttered chaos. Your main navigation should be like a well-crafted dance routine – every element is there for a reason, nothing superfluous.

Here's our tried-and-true navigation lineup:

1. Home: Your digital welcome mat. It's like the "first position" of website navigation – classic and essential.

2. About: This is where you showcase your studio's personality. Think of it as your chance to take a bow before the performance begins. Include sub-items like:

   - Our Story

   - Faculty

   - Facility

3. Classes: The main event! This is where you'll categorize your offerings. Consider sub-items such as:

   - Programs by Age

4. Reviews: Here's your chance to build social proof around your studio by showcasing your reviews from Facebook and Google.

5. Contact: Sometimes, your visitors just want to reach out and touch someone (metaphorically, of course).

   - Blog

Now, here's where we add some impact. At the top right of every page, we will place a consistent call-to-action button. It's like a key highlight in every design – impossible to ignore and designed to prompt a response.

What should this important call-to-action say? We're not revealing that just yet! Consider it the grand finale of our website makeover. But trust me, it's going to be a game-changing element that significantly boosts engagement.

Remember, your navigation should be:

- Clear: No fancy dance terms here. Use simple, straightforward language.

- Consistent: Keep the same navigation on every page. Your visitors shouldn't feel like they've stumbled into a different performance halfway through.

- Clickable: Make sure those menu items are easy to tap on mobile devices. No one should need the precision of a ballerina to navigate your site on their phone.

You're essentially creating a welcoming experience for your visitors by keeping your navigation simple and intuitive. You're saying, "Welcome! Let me guide you effortlessly through our digital space." And trust me, when it's this easy to explore your site, those visitors are much more likely to stay longer – and maybe even take the next step by becoming a student.

So, shall we move on to the next section? Remember, in the grand scheme of website design, simple navigation is your essential partner – work together seamlessly, and you'll create something truly effective.

Single, Clear Call to Action

Alright, let's talk about a crucial website element: the call-to-action (CTA). This isn't just any ordinary button – it's your website's secret weapon, the digital equivalent of your most compelling feature.

Now, remember that important button we mentioned earlier? The one positioned at the top right of every page like a key focal point? Well, we're not quite ready for the big reveal of what it says (patience is key here), but we are going to explain what happens when someone clicks it.

Here's the essential information: Your CTA should lead to one thing and one thing only – a form that asks for exactly three pieces of information. No more, no less. It's the perfect balance of data collection:

1. Name: Because it's nice to know who's joining your dance party.

2. Email: For all those digital communications.

3. Phone: Sometimes, you just need to hear a voice on the other end of the line, but even more important in 2024 and beyond… the ability to text them!

Why just these three? Well, it's like a well-executed dance move – precise, purposeful, and powerful. Asking for too much information is like adding unnecessary steps to a routine; it just complicates things and increases the chances of someone tripping up (or, in this case, clicking away).

Here's why this trio works:

- It's non-intimidating: Three fields feel manageable. It's the difference between a beginner-friendly two-step and an advanced 10-part competition routine.

- It's quick: Your visitors can fill this out faster than you can say "5-6-7-8".

- It's effective: With these three pieces of info, you've got everything you need to follow up and start turning that lead into a student.

Now, let's talk placement. This form should be prevalent throughout your site. It's like a key theme in a popular song – it should repeat often enough that people can't forget it. Have it appear when someone clicks your CTA button, of course, but also incorporate it throughout your site. At the bottom of your 'About' page? Certainly. After each class description? Absolutely. Think of it as leaving a clear path for visitors – leading straight to your studio's offerings.

Remember, the goal here isn't to gather an extensive amount of information about each prospect. It's to initiate a conversation.

Think of it as extending an invitation – you're not asking them for a major commitment, just to take the first step towards engaging with your studio.

So, while we keep you in suspense about that important CTA button's exact wording, remember this: Sometimes, less is more when gathering info. Name, email, phone – it's the perfect trio, the essential set of information for lead generation. Keep it simple, make it widely available, and watch as your website transforms into a lead-generating powerhouse that would impress even the most experienced marketers.

Color Scheme and Its Psychological Impact

Alright, color enthusiasts, it's time to choose the perfect palette for your studio's website! But before you get carried away with a wide array of digital hues, let's discuss the psychology behind colors and how they can transform your website into a lead-generating masterpiece.

Think of your color scheme as setting the mood for your digital space. It establishes the tone, creates an atmosphere, and can even influence how people perceive your studio. It's like choosing the perfect ambiance for your space – get it right, and everything else falls into place.

Here's a quick overview of the color wheel and what each hue might convey:

- Red: Passion, energy, excitement. Perfect if your studio is all about high-energy classes that get the blood pumping.

- Blue: Trust, professionalism, calm. Great for studios emphasizing technique and discipline.

- Yellow: Optimism, creativity, youth. Ideal for children's programs or studios focusing on self-expression.

- Green: Growth, harmony, health. Wonderful for studios that emphasize the wellness aspects of dance.

- Purple: Luxury, creativity, wisdom. Excellent for studios with a more artistic or avant-garde approach.

- Orange: Enthusiasm, adventure, confidence. Perfect for studios that want to appear friendly and inviting.

But wait! Before applying your chosen color across your entire site, remember this golden rule: contrast is key. You want your call-to-action buttons to stand out prominently. If your background is dark, make those buttons light (and vice versa). Your CTA should be so eye-catching that visitors' cursors are naturally drawn to it, impossible to overlook.

Now, let's talk about the psychology of color combinations:

- Complementary colors (opposite on the color wheel) create energy and make things stand out. Think blue and orange or purple and yellow.

- Analogous colors (next to each other on the color wheel) create harmony and are pleasing to the eye. Picture a gradient from blue to green to teal.

- Triadic colors (evenly spaced on the color wheel) offer vibrant contrast while maintaining harmony. Red, yellow, and blue is a classic example.

Remember, your color scheme should align with your brand personality. Are you a studio focused on traditional techniques? Softer, more muted tones might be appropriate. Running a studio that's all about energy and self-expression? Bold, vibrant colors could be just right.

Here's a pro tip: don't forget about white space! It's like a pause in a composition – it gives the eye a place to rest and can make your important elements stand out even more.

Lastly, consider color accessibility. Make sure there's enough contrast between your text and background colors. You want your website to be an experience everyone can enjoy, regardless of visual abilities.

So there you have it! Choose your palette wisely, and you'll create a website that not only looks fantastic but also psychologically primes your visitors to take that all-important next step. After all, in your website's overall presentation, color isn't just decoration – it's a key player in its own right!

Photos & Videos That Build Connection

Selecting Images that Attract New Students

Lights, camera, action! It's time to talk about the visual stars of your website – the photos and videos that will make potential students want to jump right into your studio.

First, avoid stock photos. Your website visitors can easily spot generic imagery, and it's not very appealing. What we want are authentic, vibrant visuals that capture the essence of your studio.

Capturing joy is key to images that will attract new students. Show your students mid-laugh, not just in perfect form. A genuine smile is irresistible. Show potential students that your studio is where fun and learning come together.

Your images should be varied and inclusive. Showcase students of all ages, body types, and backgrounds. Remember, every potential student should be able to look at your photos and think, "Hey, that could be me" or "That could be my child!"

While we want to show off your studio's skills, let's keep it accessible. That impressive photo of your star pupil performing an advanced move? Save it for the trophy case. Instead, opt for images that make the activity look exciting but achievable.

Give visitors a peek behind the scenes. Photos of teachers working one-on-one with students or students supporting each other during practice show the heart of your studio culture. Instead of perfectly posed performance shots, go for dynamic images that capture the energy of your classes.

Don't forget to include some shots that will resonate with the decision-makers – the parents. Images of proud family members watching performances or teachers giving encouraging high-fives can be powerful. While the focus should be on the students, a few well-chosen shots of your space can help set expectations and build excitement. Just make sure your studio is looking its best.

Remember, your goal is to make potential students (and their parents) think, "I want to be part of that!" or "My child would love it there!" Your images should tell the story of your studio – one of growth, community, and excitement.

Pro tip: Invest in a professional photographer for at least some of your shots. The difference between amateur and professional photos can be significant.

So, put on your photographer's hat and start curating a collection of images that will have new students rushing to your sign-up page. After all, in the world of studio websites, a picture isn't just worth a thousand words – it's worth a studio full of eager new students.

Importance of Smiling Faces

Let's face facts: when it comes to attracting new students, a smile is your secret weapon. We're not talking about those forced "say cheese" grins – we mean genuine, ear-to-ear, I'm-having-the-time-of-my-life smiles that are more contagious than the latest social media trend.

Smiling faces are crucial for several reasons. They create emotional contagion – smiles are catching! When potential students (and their parents) see images of happy participants, they subconsciously want to join in on the fun. It's like your photos are saying, "This is your joy. Come and claim it!"

A genuine smile builds trust quickly. It shows that your studio is a place where people feel comfortable, supported, and happy. Parents are more likely to entrust their children to a studio that radiates positivity. Smiles also make the activity look accessible. Let's face it: your craft can look intimidating to newcomers. But a smiling student says, "Don't worry, you've got this!" It makes your studio appear welcoming and inclusive rather than exclusive or overly serious.

A smile tells a story. It says, "I'm learning, I'm growing, and I'm loving every minute of it." That's a narrative that sells itself. In the sea of serious poses and intense concentration shots, images of joyful students stand out. They're the ones visitors will remember long after they've clicked away from your site.

When it comes to capturing those million-dollar smiles, remember that candid is king. Some of the best smiles happen when students don't know they're being photographed. Capture those spontaneous moments of joy during class, rehearsals, or events. You can also create smile-worthy moments by setting up fun, interactive moments during photo shoots. Have students tell jokes, play games, or reminisce about funny studio moments.

While smiles are great, don't be afraid to show other positive emotions too. Determination, excitement, and pride – these all tell important parts of the learning journey story. Look for genuine smiles that reach the eyes; those crinkles at the corners are worth their weight in gold. And don't forget about group dynamics – there's something magical about shared joy. Capture moments of students laughing together or celebrating each other's successes.

Remember, your goal is to create an emotional connection through your images. You want potential students to look at your photos and think, "I want to feel that way too!" A picture of a perfectly executed move might impress, but a photo of a beaming student mastering a new skill will inspire.

So, let's turn those frowns upside down (unless you're doing a very serious piece, of course). Fill your website with images that radiate joy, and watch as new students are drawn to your studio like moths to a particularly happy flame. After all, in your field, a smile might just be the most powerful move of all!

Using Organic-Looking Photos

Let's get real for a moment – and by real, I mean really organic. In the world of studio websites, authenticity is key. We're not talking about organic as in pesticide-free (though that's great, too); we're talking about photos that look natural, unforced, and genuinely representative of your studio's atmosphere.

Why go organic? Because today's web-savvy visitors can spot a staged, overly polished photo quickly. To keep it real and reap the rewards, focus on capturing the moment, not the pose. Instead of having students freeze in picture-perfect positions, catch them in action. A slightly blurred shot of a student mid-movement often feels more alive than a static, posed position.

Embrace imperfection. Not every hair needs to be in place; not every outfit needs to be wrinkle-free. A bit of messiness adds character and relatability. Remember, you're selling joy and growth, not perfection. Go behind the scenes and show the process, not just the final product. Shots of students preparing, helping each other, or chatting before class all add to the authentic feel.

Natural lighting is your friend. Whenever possible, use natural light. It's flattering, warm, and gives photos that genuine, slice-of-life quality. If you must use artificial lighting, aim for soft, diffused light that mimics natural illumination. While some posed shots are necessary, prioritize candid photos. They capture genuine emotions and interactions that staged photos often miss.

Don't just focus on the "pretty" parts. A photo of students cleaning up after class or working through a challenging routine shows dedication and teamwork. When it comes to post-processing, less is more. Light touch-ups are fine, but avoid heavy filters or extensive retouching that makes photos look artificial.

Ensure your photos represent the diversity of your studio. Different ages, body types, and skill levels all contribute to an organic, inclusive feel. Capture genuine interactions – photos of students laughing together, instructors giving individualized attention, or parents watching proudly from the sidelines all add to the authentic studio atmosphere.

Sometimes, the best photos are the ones you think you'll throw away – a stumble, a laugh, a moment of confusion. These can be gold for showing the real, human side of your activities.

Remember, the goal is to make potential students (and their parents) feel like they're getting a genuine peek into studio life. You want them to think, "I can see myself (or my child) there!" rather than "Wow, that looks intimidatingly perfect."

So, next time you're planning a photo shoot, think less "professional model" and more "Day in the Life of Our Studio." Keep it real and organic, and watch as your authenticity draws in new students like bees to a particularly genuine-looking flower. After all, in your field as in life, it's the unscripted moments that often create the most beautiful pictures.

Avoiding Overly Complex or Intimidating Poses

Alright, let's have a heart-to-heart about those jaw-dropping, seemingly impossible poses and movements. You know the ones – feats that make you wonder how they're even humanly possible. While these are undoubtedly impressive, they might not be your best bet for attracting new students.

Remember, your goal is to attract newcomers, not intimidate them. A photo of a student performing an extremely advanced move might make potential students think, "Wow, I could never do that," instead of, "That looks like fun!" Most of your potential students (or their parents) aren't looking to join a professional troupe. They want to learn, have fun, and improve. Show them skills and movements they can aspire to in the near future, not in ten years.

Instead of showcasing only your most advanced students, show participants at various skill levels. This demonstrates that your studio is a place for growth and improvement, not just a showcase for prodigies. There's an elegance in simplicity. A perfectly executed basic movement can be just as captivating as a complex one. Plus, it's more relatable for beginners.

Consider capturing students in motion rather than holding difficult poses. A dynamic photo of a student mid-movement often conveys more energy and excitement than a static, complex pose. Show students working together, supporting each other, or in group formations. This emphasizes the community aspect of your studio, which can be very appealing to newcomers.

Include photos of instructors demonstrating techniques or helping students. This shows that your studio is a place of learning and support, not just performance. A photo of a smiling student doing a simple move can be more inviting than a serious-faced student in a complex position. Remember, you're selling happiness as much as skills.

If you're targeting beginners or young children, your photo choices should reflect that. Save the more advanced skills for sections of your site dedicated to competitive or advanced programs. If you want to show more advanced techniques, consider creating a series of photos showing the progression from beginner to advanced. This can inspire without intimidating.

Remember, your website photos should say, "Come join us, you'll fit right in!" not "This is an elite academy for future professionals only." By choosing skills and shots that are impressive yet achievable, you create an inviting atmosphere that encourages potential students to take that first step into your studio.

So, let's keep those extremely advanced moves for the recital programs and fill your website with images that make your activities look accessible, enjoyable, and just challenging enough to be exciting. After all, every expert started as a beginner. Show your potential students where they can start, and they'll be more likely to imagine where they might end up!

Leverage Social Proof to Boost Confidence

Integrating Social Media Reviews

Social proof packs more punch than any advanced technique in the digital world. When potential students and their parents choose a studio, they're not just looking at your skills — they're tuning into what others say about you. It's time to turn your social media reviews into your most enthusiastic supporters.

The power of real voices can't be overstated. Nothing sells your studio quite like the genuine enthusiasm of your current students and their families. These social media reviews provide authentic, relatable testimonials that resonate deeply with potential students. But remember, the key is to curate, not fabricate. Choose reviews highlighting different aspects of your studio — from great instructors and a fun atmosphere to impressive student progress. Just don't be tempted to create fake reviews; it has a way of catching up!

When it comes to presenting these reviews, think visually. Don't just copy and paste text. Create eye-catching quote graphics that incorporate your brand colors and fonts. A well-designed review can catch the eye and make a lasting impression. And don't forget to showcase diversity in your reviews—include feedback from a range of students across different ages, skill levels, and styles. This demonstrates that your studio truly has something for everyone.

Keep your social proof fresh by regularly updating your featured reviews. This shows that you're consistently delivering great experiences. As for placement, don't relegate reviews to a single testimonial page. Sprinkle them throughout your site where they're most relevant. That glowing review about your specific program? It's perfect for that program's page!

When possible, link reviews back to their original source on social media. This adds an extra layer of credibility and allows potential students to explore further. While you're at it, why not create a culture of feedback? Encourage your students and their families to share their experiences on social media.

Don't panic if you get a less-than-stellar review. Address it professionally and use it as an opportunity to show how you handle feedback and continuously improve. Remember, transparency builds trust.

Think beyond just words, too. Shares, likes, and follows can also be powerful indicators of your studio's popularity and quality. If you can, include video reviews—seeing and hearing a happy student or parent can be incredibly impactful. And don't forget to highlight achievements mentioned in reviews, like a student's progress or a competition win. These success stories can be particularly motivating for potential students.

Integrating social media reviews isn't just about showing off—it's about building trust and confidence in your studio. When potential students see others raving about their experiences, they're more likely to think, "Hey, I want to be part of that!" So, start collecting those digital endorsements and turn them into your secret weapon. After all, word-of-mouth has gone digital in the world of studios, and your social media reviews are doing the work of bringing new students to your sign-up page!

Using Organic Photos in Reviews

When it comes to reviews, words pack a punch, but pairing them with authentic photos of real parents? That's the showstopper that'll have potential students and their families signing up quickly!

Picture this: a glowing review about your studio, accompanied by a photo of Sarah from the local PTA, someone your prospects might actually recognize from school pick-ups or community events. Suddenly, that review isn't just another anonymous recommendation – it's a trusted neighbor vouching for your studio.

By pulling actual photos from parents' social media reviews, you're not just sharing opinions; you're showcasing familiar faces from the community. This approach transforms your testimonials from distant praise to personal endorsements. It's like having a friend recommend your studio personally.

The beauty of using these genuine parent photos lies in their authenticity. We're not talking about polished headshots or professional portraits. Instead, think of the everyday photos people use on their social profiles – a casual selfie, a family picnic snapshot, or a proud parent moment at a performance. These real-life images resonate because they're relatable and genuine.

This strategy also builds a sense of community around your studio. When prospects see parents they recognize praising your classes, it creates a powerful connection. It's social proof in its purest form – "If it's good enough for Sarah's kids, it might be perfect for mine too!"

Remember, diversity is key. Showcase a range of parents from different backgrounds, age groups, and family structures. This reinforces the message that your studio is a welcoming place for all families in your community.

By using genuine parent photos in your reviews, you're not just telling potential students about the great experiences they could have at your studio – you're showing them through the eyes of people they know and trust. You're inviting them to join a community, not just a class. So go ahead, let those familiar faces shine. After all, in the world of studio marketing, there's no endorsement more powerful than that of a satisfied parent from your own neighborhood.

Keeping visitors on your site

In the digital age, studio prospects are like savvy online shoppers – they want to see reviews before making a decision. The key to converting these prospects into students is keeping them on your website by providing all the social proof they need right there.

Instead of linking to external review sites or social media platforms, bring those valuable reviews directly onto your website. By integrating real parent and student reviews, complete with their photos and experiences, you satisfy your prospects' need for research without the risk of losing them to another site.

This approach serves two crucial purposes: it provides the authentic feedback prospects are looking for, and it eliminates any reason for them to click away from your site. When all the positive experiences and community endorsements are right there on your pages, prospects can easily build confidence in your studio without the temptation to look elsewhere.

Remember, every click away from your site is a potential lost student. By keeping reviews and testimonials in-house, you're not just providing information – you're guiding your prospects smoothly towards that all-important sign-up form.

In essence, your website becomes a one-stop-shop for both information and validation, keeping potential students engaged and moving them closer to joining your community. It's about creating a seamless experience that transforms curious clicks into committed students, all without ever leaving your digital space.

Creating a dedicated reviews page

Let's talk about the powerhouse of your studio website - the reviews page. Our data from managing thousands of websites shows it's often the second most visited page on a studio site. It's where potential students and their parents go to get the real scoop on your studio.

The key to making this page irresistible? Embed authentic reviews directly from social media platforms like Facebook and Google. These carry extra weight because they require real profiles to post, making them the gold standard of authenticity in the eyes of your prospects.

Create a wall of these embedded reviews that's so impressive, so overwhelming in its positivity, that it makes your studio the clear, undeniable choice. We're talking about a reviews page that your competitors couldn't recreate if they tried for years.

The process is simple but powerful:

1. Collect and embed every positive review from your Facebook page and Google Business profile.

2. Include the reviewer's profile picture (which comes automatically with the embedded review) to add a face to the praise.

The beauty of this approach is twofold. First, it's undeniably authentic. Prospects can see these are real people from their community, not just testimonials you've written yourself. Second, it's dynamic. As new reviews come in on these platforms, they'll automatically appear on your page, keeping it fresh and current.

Organize these embedded reviews in a visually appealing way. Create a mosaic of positive experiences that prospects can scroll through, each one reinforcing your studio's excellence.

Remember, quantity matters here. We're aiming for a wall of positivity so extensive that it becomes undeniable. When a prospect scrolls through dozens upon dozens of genuine, enthusiastic reviews pulled directly from trusted social platforms, the decision to choose your studio becomes a no-brainer.

By creating this dedicated page of embedded social media reviews, you're not just sharing feedback - you're showcasing irrefutable proof of your studio's impact and excellence. It's a powerful tool that sets you apart from the competition and turns curious clicks into committed students.

Age-Based Class Pages for Clarity

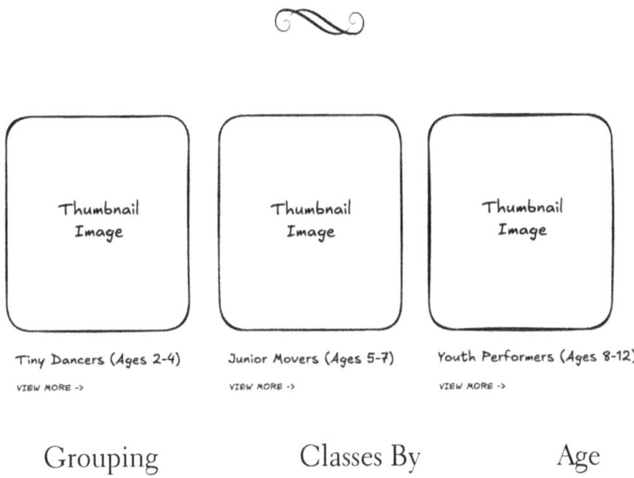

Grouping   Classes By   Age

Let's face it: many studio websites are like an overly complex food menu - overwhelming, confusing, and likely to induce decision paralysis. But here's the thing: when it comes to your website, simpler is always better. We're not here to confuse; we're here to convert.

The solution? Age-based class pages. It's a simple concept that can dramatically improve your website's user experience and, ultimately, your enrollment numbers. Here's why it works:

Every prospect knows one crucial piece of information: their age (or their child's age). It's the most straightforward way for them to narrow down their options and find relevant classes. By organizing your classes by age group, you're essentially holding your prospect's hand and guiding them directly to the information they need.

Instead of a single, intimidating page listing every technique and program you offer, break it down into age-specific categories. For example:

- Tiny Dancers (Ages 2-4)
- Junior Movers (Ages 5-7)
- Youth Performers (Ages 8-12)
- Teen Dancers (Ages 13-17)
- Adult Classes (18+)

Each of these should be a separate page, easily accessible from your main navigation bar. List them as sub-items under your "Classes" menu item. This structure allows visitors to quickly find and click on the age group that applies to them.

But don't stop there. Feature these age-based categories prominently on your homepage as well. Create visually appealing thumbnails or buttons for each age group, making it easy for visitors to dive right into the relevant information from the moment they land on your site.

Within each age-specific page, you can then list the various styles and levels available for that age group. This approach not only simplifies the user experience but also allows you to tailor your messaging and imagery to each specific age group.

Remember, the goal is to make it as easy as possible for prospects to find what they're looking for. By grouping classes by age, you're eliminating confusion, streamlining the decision-making process, and ultimately increasing the likelihood of turning visitors into students.

In the world of studio websites, less really is more. So, let's opt for a clean, simple menu that guides prospects effortlessly to their perfect class. After all, the easier you make it for them to find what they want, the more likely they are to take that crucial next step and sign up for a class.

Creating Age Specific Funnels

Now that we've sorted our classes into age-specific pages, it's time to transform these pages into powerful, targeted funnels. Remember, each age group comes with its own set of challenges, desires, and needs. Your job is to speak directly to these, positioning your studio as the perfect solution.

Keep in mind that the age groups and class names we'll discuss are just examples. You should customize these to fit your specific studio's offerings and target demographics. The key is to create distinct categories that make sense for your programs and clientele.

Let's break it down using some example age groups:

For the youngest students: Focus on early developmental benefits. Discuss how your activities improve motor skills, encourage social interaction, and provide a fun outlet for boundless energy. Parents of toddlers are often looking for activities that are both fun and educational. Highlight how your classes foster creativity, teach basic listening skills, and help with coordination.

For elementary school-aged children: Emphasize how your classes help kids build confidence, make new friends, and discover their passions. Talk about the joy of self-expression and how your activities can be a positive outlet for emotions.

For preteens and early teens: This is often when interests start to get more serious for those who love them. Discuss how your classes can help channel their growing passion, improve skills, and provide opportunities for performance or showcases. Mention how your activities can be a great way to stay active, build discipline, and boost self-esteem during these crucial developmental years.

For older teens: Position your activities as a healthy outlet for stress, a way to stay fit, and a place to belong. Discuss how your classes can help build lifelong friendships, provide a sense of accomplishment, and even open doors to potential career paths.

For adults: Adults have varied reasons for joining - fitness, social interaction, stress relief, or fulfilling a lifelong dream. Address all these motivations. Talk about how your classes offer a fun alternative to the gym, a way to meet like-minded people, and an opportunity to challenge oneself. Emphasize that it's never too late to start.

For each age group, include those organic, authentic photos we discussed earlier. Show real students of the appropriate age group in action - laughing, participating, and clearly enjoying themselves. This helps potential students and parents envision themselves or their children in your studio.

Throughout each page, include your consistent call-to-action multiple times. While we'll reveal the specific wording later, remember that it should be prominent and easy to spot.

By tailoring each page to the specific needs and desires of different age groups, you're creating targeted funnels that speak directly to your prospects. This personalized approach shows that you understand and can meet their unique needs, making your studio the clear choice. Remember, in the world of studio marketing, the more personal and relevant you can make your message, the more likely you are to transform curious visitors into enthusiastic new students.

Community Recognition & Awards

Showcasing Studio Achievements

When it comes to showcasing your studio's achievements, it's time to shift focus towards your community's impact. While competitive awards are impressive, your local reputation and community involvement truly resonate with potential students and their families.

Focus on the accolades that demonstrate your studio's standing in the community. These are the awards that show you're not just teaching great skills, but you're also an integral part of the local fabric. We're talking about honors like:

- "Best of [Your City Name]" awards
- "Readers' Choice" recognitions from local publications
- Chamber of Commerce acknowledgments
- Local business excellence awards

These types of commendations speak volumes about your studio's reputation for customer service, overall experience, and community engagement. They signal to potential students that your studio is trusted, respected, and beloved by the very community they live in.

Remember, parents and adult students seek more than just technical instruction. They want a welcoming environment, excellent customer service, and a sense of belonging. These community awards are proof that you deliver on all fronts.

Don't be shy about displaying these accolades prominently on your website. Create a dedicated section or banner that showcases these awards. Use the official logos of the awarding organizations if possible, as they lend additional credibility.

In addition to community awards, highlight any local media coverage your studio has received. If you've been featured on local news stations or in newspaper articles, display those media logos on your site. Whether it was a video segment about your annual showcase or a written piece about your community outreach program, this coverage borrows credibility from established media sources.

For maximum impact, place a banner or footer with these awards and media logos on every page of your website. This consistent presence reinforces your studio's standing and sets you apart from competitors at every turn.

Remember, you're the only studio in your area that can claim these specific community accolades. They're unique differentiators that immediately elevate your studio in the eyes of prospects.

By showcasing these community recognitions and media features, you're telling potential students and their families, "We're not just here to create great performers. We're here to be a great member of our community." This approach positions your studio as more than just a place to learn skills – it's a local institution that people trust and value.

So, let those community awards and media mentions take center stage on your website. They're your not-so-secret weapons in converting visitors into students. After all, who wouldn't want to be part of a studio that their whole community already knows and loves?

Highlighting Community Involvement

Awards are fantastic, but truly being a community asset is where the real magic happens. It's not just about talking the talk; it's about walking the walk of community engagement. Let's explore how your studio can become an integral part of your local fabric and showcase these efforts on your website.

There are numerous ways to contribute to your community:

1. Educational Support: Donate to your local school board or sponsor school events. This shows your commitment to education beyond dance.

2. Volunteering: Engage your staff and students in local volunteer efforts. Whether it's cleaning up a park or

serving at a soup kitchen, these activities demonstrate your studio's values in action.

3. Silent Auctions: Donate class packages or performance tickets to charity silent auctions. It's a win-win: you support a good cause and introduce your studio to potential new students.

4. Local Fairs and Events: Set up a booth at community fairs. Offer something free, like cotton candy or mini dance lessons. It's a great way to interact with the community in a fun, pressure-free environment.

5. Parade Participation: Be a part of local parades. Your dancers can showcase their skills while providing entertainment for the community.

6. Benefit Performances: Organize performances to raise funds for local charities. It gives your students a chance to shine while supporting important causes.

7. Workshop Series: Offer free dance workshops in public spaces like parks or community centers. It's a great way to introduce dance to those who might not otherwise have access.

These activities do more than just build goodwill; they build your brand. The more involved you are in the community, the more people will visit your website to learn about your studio. And as we've discussed before, more website visitors mean more potential students.

But don't stop at just doing these activities – showcase them on your website! Create a dedicated "Community Involvement" page where you highlight your various contributions. Use this page to share stories, photos, and even testimonials from community partners about the impact of your involvement.

Additionally, leverage your website's blog to create content around these community efforts. Write posts about your experiences at local events, share photos from your volunteer days, or spotlight student involvement in community service. This approach serves multiple purposes:

1. It demonstrates your community's commitment to website visitors.

2. It provides fresh, engaging content for your current dance families.

3. It helps with search engine optimization and improves your site's visibility in local searches.

Remember, every blog post about your community involvement is an opportunity to reinforce your studio's values and connect with potential students on a deeper level.

By actively engaging in and highlighting your community involvement, you're showing that your studio is more than just a business – it's a valued community partner. This not only sets you apart from competitors but also creates an emotional connection with potential students and their families. After all, people are more likely to choose a studio that teaches great skills and contributes to making their community a better place.

So, step out into your community with enthusiasm and purpose. Then, make sure to showcase these efforts on your website. It's a powerful way to demonstrate your values, build your brand, and, ultimately, bring more students through your studio doors.

Position your studio as a community asset

While this book is primarily about creating a stellar website for your studio, it's crucial to understand that your studio's role in the community directly impacts your online presence. Being a true community asset isn't just good for your neighborhood—it's a powerful strategy for driving organic traffic to your website.

Think of your community involvement as the key that launches your studio into the spotlight. When you position your studio as a valuable community asset, you create buzz, build trust, and generate interest that naturally leads people to your website. And as we know, more website visitors mean more potential students.

To solidify your position as a community asset, be consistently present at local events. Regular involvement in community gatherings keeps your studio top-of-mind. Whether it's annual parades, seasonal festivals, or charity runs, make sure your studio is there, contributing positively.

Offer value beyond your primary services by hosting free workshops on relevant topics. These events position your studio as a source of valuable information, not just instruction. Partner with local businesses for cross-promotion, expanding your reach and strengthening your local business network.

Support local causes by aligning your studio with charities or community initiatives. This could involve fundraising performances or donation drives, showing that your studio cares about issues that matter to your community. Open your doors to host community events at your studio, positioning it as a hub for community activity.

Engage with schools by offering after-school programs or collaborating on their events. This builds relationships with educators and families. Share your expertise by writing columns for local publications or appearing on local radio shows to discuss relevant topics, positioning you as a local expert.

When you engage in these activities, you're not just building goodwill—you're creating stories, experiences, and reasons for people to visit your website. They'll want to learn more about the studio that's making such a positive impact in their community.

Remember, every community activity is an opportunity to direct people to your website for more information. Make sure your web address is on all materials distributed at community events. Encourage people to visit your site to learn more about your programs or to see photos from community events.

By positioning your studio as a vital community asset, you create a powerful ripple effect. Your community involvement generates interest and goodwill, which drives traffic to your website and helps convert visitors into students. It's a virtuous cycle that benefits your studio, students, and community.

In essence, being a community asset is about more than just doing good—it's a strategic approach to growing your studio. It's about creating a presence in your community that's so positive and impactful that people are naturally drawn to learn more about you. And where do they go to learn more? Your website, of course.

So, as you work on perfecting your website, remember that your real-world community involvement is the secret ingredient that will drive people to visit it. By being a true community asset, you're not just building a better neighborhood—you're building a stronger, more successful studio.

SECTION 6

Setting Your Studio Apart

Introducing Your Faculty

Your faculty isn't just a group of instructors – they're the heart and soul of your studio, the mentors who will shape your students' journeys. Introducing them properly on your website is a golden opportunity to build trust, showcase expertise, and create a personal connection with prospective students and their families.

Start with high-quality, professional photos of each staff member. These aren't stuffy corporate headshots – we want warm, inviting images that capture each instructor's personality. Aim for uniformity in style – perhaps all instructors in appropriate attire against a consistent background. The key is to ensure everyone looks approachable and friendly. Remember, a smile goes a long way in making prospective students feel welcome before they even step foot in your studio.

Alongside each photo, include the instructor's name and role. But don't stop there – this is your chance to bring each faculty member to life. Share a brief bio highlighting their background, teaching philosophy, and perhaps a personal touch that makes them unique. Did Julie study under a renowned expert? Does

Tom have a knack for calming nervous beginners? These details help paint a picture of the people behind the instruction.

Consider including information such as:

- Years of dance experience

- Areas of expertise (ballet, hip-hop, contemporary, etc.)

- Notable performances or competitions

- Teaching certifications or special training

- A quote about their teaching philosophy or love for dance

You might also include a fun fact or two about each instructor. Maybe Sarah is an avid rock climber, or John makes incredible cupcakes. These personal touches help humanize your instructors and can create points of connection with prospective students.

If space allows, consider adding a short video introduction from each instructor. This gives visitors a chance to see your faculty in action and get a sense of their teaching style and personality.

Remember, the goal here is to showcase your studio's unique expertise while also building a sense of warmth and accessibility. You want prospective students to think, "Wow, these instructors really know their stuff – and they seem like people I'd enjoy learning from!"

By introducing your faculty in a personal, engaging way, you're not just listing credentials – you're inviting prospective students into your studio family. You're showing them the faces they'll see each week, the expertise they'll benefit from, and the personalities that make your studio special.

This personal touch can be the deciding factor for many prospects. In a sea of studios, it's often the human element that sets you apart. So let your faculty shine, and watch as prospective students are drawn to the unique culture and expertise that only your studio can offer.

Presenting your mission and values

In the world of studios, skill and talent are just the beginning. What truly sets you apart is your 'why' – the driving force behind every lesson and performance. As Simon Sinek famously said in his book "Start with Why," people don't buy what you do; they buy why you do it. This principle is the secret sauce to building a studio that doesn't just teach techniques but inspires passion and loyalty.

Your mission statement is the heartbeat of your studio. It's not just a collection of fancy words but a clear, concise declaration of why your studio exists. Are you here to nurture creativity in young minds? To build confidence through your craft? To preserve and promote a particular tradition? Whatever your mission, state it boldly and let it shine through every aspect of your website.

Equally important are your studio's values. These are the principles that guide your decisions, shape your culture, and define what you stand for. Do you value inclusivity, pushing boundaries, or maintaining traditions? Are you all about fostering a supportive community or driving competitive excellence? Your values should be clear, authentic, and reflected in everything from your class structure to your showcase philosophy.

When presenting your mission and values on your website, consider these tips:

1. Make it prominent: Don't bury your mission statement. Feature it prominently, perhaps on your 'About Us' page.

2. Use compelling language: Your mission and values should inspire and excite. Use language that's passionate and authentic to your studio's personality.

3. Show, don't just tell: Illustrate your values in action. Use photos, reviews, or short videos that demonstrate how your mission and values play out in real studio life.

4. Connect it to your offerings: Explain how your mission and values influence your teaching methods, class structure, and overall student experience.

5. Be specific about what makes you unique: Highlight the aspects of your studio that stem directly from your mission and values. Maybe it's your inclusive approach, your emphasis on history and context, or your commitment to community performances.

6. Encourage alignment: Invite prospective students and parents who resonate with your mission to join your studio

family. This self-selection helps ensure you attract students who will thrive in your unique culture.

Remember, your mission and values are not just for show – they should be the driving force behind every decision you make. When you authentically present these core principles, you attract students and families who share your passion and vision. This alignment creates a strong, supportive community that goes beyond just taking classes.

By clearly articulating your 'why,' you're not just selling lessons; you're offering an opportunity to be part of something meaningful. In a world where people crave connection and purpose, a studio with a strong sense of mission can be a beacon, attracting students who are looking for more than just technique but a place to belong and grow.

So, let your mission and values take center stage on your website. They're the foundation of your unique culture, the magnet that will attract your ideal students, and the fuel that will keep your studio thriving for years to come.

Attracting Ideal Customers

Let's face it: not all students (or parents) are created equal when it comes to aligning with your studio's culture. The last thing you want is a studio filled with families who don't share your values, are consistently late, struggle with payments, or simply don't appreciate what you offer. Your website is your first line of defense – and your best tool – for attracting your ideal community.

Your website should act as a magnet, drawing in those who resonate with your studio's ethos while gently steering away those who might not be the best fit. Here's how to use your site to attract your dream studio family:

Be unapologetically you: Don't water down your studio's personality or values to appeal to everyone. If you're all about disciplined training, say so. If you prioritize fun and self-expression over perfection, make that clear. The right students will be drawn to your authenticity.

Showcase your community: Share stories, photos, and testimonials from current students and parents who embody your ideal. This gives prospects a clear picture of the type of community they'll be joining.

Highlight your unique approach: If you have a particular teaching philosophy or studio culture, explain it in detail. This could be anything from your showcase policies to your approach to skill development.

Use language that resonates with your ideal customers: The tone and style of your website copy should speak directly to the type of families you want to attract. If you're aiming for serious, dedicated students, your language might be more formal and focused on achievement. If you're all about inclusive, joyful learning, let that shine through in a more casual, upbeat tone.

Create content that aligns with your values: Blog posts, videos, or social media content shared on your site should reflect your studio's priorities. If you value technical excellence, share tips for improving skills. If community is key, showcase your studio's involvement in local events.

Be clear about what makes you different: Don't be afraid to differentiate yourself from other studios. If you don't focus on competitions, say so. If you have a unique curriculum or teaching method, explain why you believe in it.

Remember, your goal isn't to appeal to everyone – it's to create a strong connection with the right people. By clearly communicating your studio's culture, values, and expectations through your website, you're more likely to attract students and families who will thrive in your environment.

This approach might mean turning away some potential customers, but that's okay. In the long run, you'll build a studio community that's aligned, supportive, and a joy to work with. You'll spend less time dealing with conflicts or misunderstandings and more time doing what you love – teaching students who truly appreciate your unique approach.

Your website is more than just an information hub; it's a powerful tool for shaping your studio's culture and community. Use it wisely to attract your ideal tribe, and watch as your studio flourishes with students and families who share your passion, respect your values, and contribute positively to your studio family.

The Missing Link for 98% of Dance Studios

Don't display your pricing and schedule

Let's address the elephant in the room – or rather, the information conspicuously absent from your website. We're talking about pricing and schedules, the two pieces of information that 98% of studios mistakenly put front and center on their websites. But here's the twist: keeping this information off your site could be the game-changer your studio needs.

Why? Because most prospects who land on your website are initially fixated on two things: how much it costs and when classes are held. They're ready to make snap judgments based on these factors alone, potentially disqualifying themselves before they've had a chance to see the true value your studio offers.

Think about it. You've poured your heart and soul into creating an exceptional program. You've cultivated a unique studio culture, assembled a top-notch faculty, and become a pillar of your community. Your website beautifully showcases all of this – your classes, achievements, and values. But by immediately providing pricing and schedules, you're inviting prospects to skip over all that rich content and make a decision based solely on numbers.

Here's the problem with that approach:

1. Dance studio pricing can be complex. Without context, a price point might seem high to someone who doesn't understand the value they're getting.

2. Schedules, when viewed in isolation, might not align perfectly with a prospect's ideal scenario, causing them to click away without exploring alternatives.

3. By focusing on these details upfront, prospects miss out on the emotional connection they could be forming with your studio's unique offerings and culture.

Instead of displaying this information openly, use it as leverage to start a conversation. Make your call-to-action about requesting pricing and schedule information. This approach offers several benefits:

1. It encourages prospects to engage with your other content first, allowing them to understand the full value of what you're offering.

2. It provides you with lead information, allowing you to follow up personally.

3. It gives you the opportunity to explain your pricing structure and explore scheduling options in a way that highlights the value and flexibility of your program.

4. It allows you to directly address any concerns or questions, improving the chances of converting a prospect into a student.

Remember, your goal is to build a relationship, not just relay information. By withholding pricing and schedules, you're not being coy – you're creating an opportunity for dialogue. You're saying, "Let's talk about what you're looking for in a studio, and I'll show you how we can meet those needs."

This approach might feel counterintuitive at first. You might worry that you'll frustrate potential customers by not providing this information upfront. But in reality, you're doing them a service by ensuring they have all the context they need to make an informed decision.

So, take a deep breath and remove those pricing tables and calendar widgets from your site. Replace them with compelling calls-to-action that invite prospects to reach out for more information. Then, watch as your lead quality improves and your conversion rates soar. After all, in the process of customer acquisition, sometimes the most powerful move is the one you don't make.

Using pricing and schedule information as a call-to-action

The moment has arrived to unveil the secret weapon I've been hinting at throughout this book. It's time to talk about the most powerful call-to-action (CTA) you can have on your studio website. Drum roll, please...

Your primary CTA, the one that should be prominently displayed in the top right corner of every single page on your website, should simply read: "Schedule & Pricing."

But here's where the magic happens. This button doesn't lead to a page displaying your schedule and prices. Instead, it opens a form requesting the visitor's name, email, and phone number.

Similarly, throughout your website, wherever you've placed a CTA (and remember, we recommend multiple instances per page), it should read: "View our schedule & pricing options," followed by fields for name, email, and phone.

Why is this so effective? Because it taps into the two pieces of information that nearly every prospective student or parent is most interested in – when can they attend classes, and how much will it cost? By offering this information in exchange for contact details, you're providing value while also capturing leads.

This approach is powerful for several reasons:

1. It satisfies the visitor's primary curiosity, making them more likely to engage.

2. It creates a sense of exclusivity around your pricing and schedule information.

3. It allows you to capture lead information from highly interested prospects.

4. It opens the door for personalized follow-up, where you can highlight the value of your programs.

Implementing this CTA strategy can lead to an immediate uptick in leads and, ultimately, new student enrollments. Even if you make no other changes to your website, this one adjustment can significantly impact your conversion rates.

Remember, the goal isn't just to provide information – it's to start a conversation. By using pricing and schedule information as your primary CTA, you invite prospects to engage with you directly. This allows you to showcase your studio's unique value, address any concerns, and guide potential students towards enrollment.

So, go ahead and make this change to your website. Replace those generic "Contact Us" or "Learn More" buttons with this targeted, high-converting CTA. Watch as your lead generation soars and your studio fills with students who have already taken the first step towards becoming part of your community.

In the grand scheme of your studio's marketing strategy, this CTA is your key feature. Use it wisely, and prepare for excellent results in the form of a flood of new leads and students!

Reducing confusion for non-dance prospects

Now, you might be thinking, "Won't hiding pricing and schedules annoy my prospects?" The short answer is no, and here's why:

Put yourself in the shoes of someone who's never signed up for classes at your studio before. They're excited about the possibility, but they're also stepping into unfamiliar territory. With their array of class types, levels, and time slots, schedules can be overwhelmingly complex to the uninitiated.

Think about it: How many hours per week should a beginner take? What's the difference between various class types? Is it okay to mix styles, or should they focus on one? These are questions that experienced parents might know the answers to, but for newcomers, it's like trying to decipher a foreign language.

I've seen thousands of studio schedules, and let me tell you, they're confusing even for someone in the industry. It can be downright intimidating for a parent who's just trying to find an after-school activity for their child. It's very difficult for them to understand exactly which classes are relevant based on their child's age, interest, and experience level.

By not displaying this information upfront, you're not being evasive – you're offering a white-glove experience. You're saying, "Let us guide you through this process." When a prospect reaches out for pricing and schedule information, you have the opportunity to:

1. Understand their specific situation: Their child's age, previous dance experience (if any), and their goals.

2. Learn about their needs and desires: Are they looking for a casual, fun activity or more serious training?

3. Discuss any concerns or questions they might have about starting dance classes.

4. Make professional recommendations based on this information.

This approach allows you to tailor your response to each prospect's unique situation. Instead of leaving them to puzzle over a complex schedule and price list, you can suggest the perfect combination of classes for their needs. You can explain why certain classes are recommended and how they'll benefit the student.

Moreover, this personalized interaction allows you to showcase your studio's expertise and care right from the start. You're not just selling classes; you're providing a consultative experience that demonstrates your commitment to each student's success.

Remember, your goal isn't to confuse or frustrate prospects – it's to guide them through the process of becoming part of your studio family. By controlling the flow of information, you're able to ensure that prospects have the context they need to understand the value of your offerings.

In the end, most prospects will appreciate this personalized approach. They're not just getting raw data; they're getting expert guidance. And that, in the world of education, is invaluable.

So don't worry about annoying your prospects. Instead, focus on how you can use this opportunity to provide an exceptional, personalized experience right from their first interaction with your studio. That kind of first impression turns curious prospects into committed students.

Increasing one-on-one conversations

By withholding pricing and schedule information from your website (until they opt-in), you're opening the door to something invaluable: more one-on-one conversations with potential students and their families. In an age of digital transactions and automated responses, this personal touch can be your secret weapon.

Remember, at the end of the day, people want to do business with people, not faceless entities. By using pricing and schedule inquiries as a catalyst for direct communication, you're creating an opportunity to build relationships from the very first interaction.

Now, you might be thinking, "But doesn't this mean more work?" The short answer is yes, it does. However, running a successful business takes work, and this is work that pays off in spades.

Here's why these one-on-one conversations are worth the effort:

1. They allow you to showcase your studio's personality and values directly.

2. You can address concerns and questions immediately, increasing the likelihood of conversion.

3. You can tailor your pitch to each prospect's specific needs and situation.

4. It gives you a chance to upsell or recommend additional classes based on the conversation.

5. You're building a relationship, not just processing a transaction.

But what about the workload? Yes, it will increase initially, but consider this an investment in your studio's growth. As you start seeing the fruits of your labor in the form of new students and additional revenue, you'll be in a position to hire a dedicated admin who can be responsible for nurturing these leads.

Moreover, technology can help streamline this process. Tools like SMS/email automations and chatbots can initially do a lot of the heavy lifting for you. These can handle basic inquiries, provide general information, and even schedule calls while maintaining a personal touch. This allows you to focus your energy on the conversations that are most likely to result in new enrollments.

Here's a potential workflow:

1. Prospect requests pricing/schedule information via your website form.

2. An automated email & text message is sent with some general information and an invitation to schedule a call.

3. A chatbot can handle initial questions and gather more information about the prospect's needs.

4. You (or your admin) have a personal conversation with the well-qualified, informed prospect.

This approach allows you to scale your personal touch without becoming overwhelmed. You're providing immediate response and information to all inquiries while focusing your personal energy where it's most effective.

Remember, these conversations are not just about conveying information – they're about building relationships. They're your opportunity to turn curious prospects into enthusiastic students, address concerns before they become obstacles, and showcase the unique value your studio offers.

So embrace these one-on-one conversations. Yes, they require effort, but they are the foundation of a thriving studio. They're how you build a community, not just a customer base. In the world of education and personal development, that community is what will set your studio apart and ensure its long-term success.

Conclusion

As we wrap up our journey through the world of dance studio website optimization, let's revisit the seven key points we've covered:

1. Overall Structure: Creating a clean, intuitive layout that guides visitors effortlessly through your site.

2. Photos & Videos That Build Connection: Using authentic, engaging visuals to showcase your studio's spirit.

3. Leveraging Social Proof: Integrating genuine testimonials and reviews to build trust and credibility.

4. Age-Based Class Pages: Organizing your offerings in a way that speaks directly to each age group's needs and desires.

5. Community Recognition & Awards: Showcasing your studio's impact and standing in the local community.

6. Setting Yourself Apart with Your Unique Culture: Highlighting your studio's values, mission, and the personalities that make it special.

7. The Missing Link - Pricing and Scheduling: Using these crucial pieces of information as a tool for engagement rather than self-disqualification.

These seven elements aren't isolated strategies - they're interconnected pieces of a cohesive whole. Your overall structure provides the framework while engaging photos and videos bring it to life. Social proof builds trust, which is reinforced by your community recognition. Age-based pages speak directly to your prospects' needs, while your unique culture shows why you're the right choice. Finally, your approach to pricing and scheduling information turns casual browsers into engaged leads.

Together, these elements create a website that doesn't just inform - it connects, engages, and converts. It's a digital representation of your studio's heart and soul, designed to turn curious clicks into committed students.

Implementing these strategies has the potential to revolutionize your student enrollment. By creating a website that truly showcases your studio's value, speaks directly to your ideal students, and encourages meaningful engagement, you're setting the stage for significant growth.

Expect to see an increase in quality leads, higher conversion rates, and, ultimately, a boost in student enrollments. Moreover, because you're attracting students who align with your studio's values and approach, you're likely to see improved retention rates and a more cohesive studio community.

Now that you're armed with these powerful strategies, it's time to put them into action. You have two paths forward:

1. DIY Approach: Take this information and implement it yourself. It will require time, effort, and possibly some trial and error, but the potential results are well worth it.

2. Professional Support: If you'd prefer expert guidance and implementation, consider partnering with Market Muscles. We offer an affordable monthly service specifically designed for dance studios. We'll design your website, implement all the strategies we've discussed, and provide full-time support via phone, email, and chat. We're here to help with any adjustments or changes you need, ensuring your website continues to perform at its peak.

Want to learn more about Market Muscles? Visit us at www.marketmuscles.com/website-audit/ or scan the QR code below!

Whether you choose to go it alone or partner with us, remember this: implementing these strategies will yield massive results. Your website will transform from a simple online brochure into a powerful student recruitment tool.

The stage is yours. It's time to take your studio's online presence from a basic introduction to a showstopping performance. Your future students are out there waiting to discover the magic of your studio. With these strategies in place, you're ready to reach, engage, and welcome them into your studio family.

So, are you ready to revolutionize your studio's online presence? The spotlight's on, and it's time for your website to take center stage. Let's get started!

About the Author

Stephen Reinstein is the CEO & Founder of Market Muscles, a pioneering company dedicated to helping dance and martial arts studios thrive. With over eight years of industry experience, Stephen has established himself as a leading authority in creating innovative technology solutions that drive student enrollment and retention.

Under Stephen's leadership, Market Muscles has successfully generated over 1.5 million leads for its members, providing them with lead-generating websites and online marketing tools tailored to their unique needs. Stephen's passion for connecting more children with top-tier dance studios has been a driving force behind Market Muscles' mission and success.

Through his expertise and dedication, Stephen continues to revolutionize the way dance and martial arts studios attract and retain students, making a significant impact on the industries he serves.

Outside of his professional life, Stephen enjoys spending time with his girlfriend, family, and 3 dogs, traveling to Japan, and practicing martial arts.